S T O N E   N E S T

Paul Klee, *Plants in Moonlight*, 1922.

*where old dragons
come to rise again
before they rest*

STONE NEST

POEMS

RICHARD COLLINS

SHANTI ARTS PUBLISHING
BRUNSWICK, MAINE

STONE NEST

Published by Shanti Arts Publishing
Designed by Shanti Arts Designs

Cover image: Paul Klee, *Plants in Moonlight*, 1922.
© 2025 Artists Rights Society (ARS), New York

Shanti Arts LLC
193 Hillside Road
Brunswick, Maine 04011
shantiarts.com

Printed in the United States of America

ISBN: 978-1-962082-99-0 (softcover)

Library of Congress Control Number: 2025946466

In memory of my mentors
Robert Peters (1924–2014) and
Robert Reibin Livingston Roshi (1933–2021)

and in gratitude to
Lana Matthews Sain
and my other students, past and present

Contents

SHORELESS RIVER

CODA

ACKNOWLEDGMENTS

Thanks to the editors of the following journals who published these poems in their original forms:

Alien Buddha Zine: "Formless Merit" and "The Zen Monk to His Designer Dog" (2024)

Amethyst Review: "Mi Fu Bowing to the Stone"; "Nighttime Thoughts on the Mountain"; and "A Bat in the Pantry" (2025)

Blue Unicorn: "The Next Generation" (2024)

The Braided Way: "The Hermit Puts Out a Mission Statement" (2025)

Buckle &: "Something for Su Tungpo" (1999)

The Dead Mule School of Southern Literature: "Cement Buddha" and "The Past Is Not Past in Sewanee, Tennessee" (2024)

Exquisite Corpse: "Old Poet, Old Frogs" (from "Bodhidharma's Eyelids") (2001–2002)

Five Fleas: "Yes, Emptiness" (2025)

The Gilded Weathervane: "Deep Spring Rain Has Passed" and "Returning to Live in the South" (Farm Girls Press, 2025)

High Rise: Brutalist Poetry: "The Man in the Blue Wheelchair" (The Broken Spine: Thematic Slimline Poetry Anthologies, 2025)

Ink Nest Poetry: "Riding and Writing in Circles" (2025)

Lindenwood Review: "If we win the lottery or are reincarnated . . . " (2025)

Littoral Magazine: "I Climb Stone Nest in Silence"; "Semis Climb the Mountain Road"; "The Shock of Recognition"; and "The Teacher Keeps His Counsel" (2024)

Locust Shells Journal: "Carapaces" (nominated for Best of the Net 2026) (2025)

Marrow Magazine: "Daruma Gets His Ears Cleaned" (2024)

MockingHeart Review: "Out with the Old" (2024)

The Orchards Poetry Journal: "Idle in the Study, Winter, With Dogs" (2024)

Paper Dragon: "Written for the Backyard Naturalist from Maine" (2024)

Pensive: A Global Journal of Spirituality: "There's Something about Bamboo" (2024)

Poem Alone: "No Longer Drunk on the Road at Night" (2024)

Prosetrics: "Cacti in the Cabin Window" (2025)

The Seventh Quarry (Wales): "Seventy-Three" (2025)

Shō Poetry Journal: "Petrichor"; "Remembering Reibin"; "Shoreless River"; and "Wind Flows Over Stone Nest Dojo" (nominated for Best Spiritual Literature) (2023–2024)

Shot Glass: "As Unattached as Leaves in October"; "Postcard: Returning from Arizona in June"; and "Still Lifes Everywhere" (2024)

Synaeresis: art + poetry: "From Stone Nest to the Sunflowers" (2024)

Think Journal: "Collecting the Mail" and "Hiking Fiery Gizzard" (2024)

Urthona: Buddhism and the Arts: "In the Posture of the Water Dragon" and "Leaving the Abbot Behind" (2024)

Willows Wept Review: "The Changing Light at Stone Nest"; "Insinuations of Summer"; and "The Samadhi of Words" (nominated for Pushcart Prize) (2024)

Writing the Drought: A Collection of Poems by Kern County Authors: "Blood, Sweat, and Petrichor" (2016)

Xavier Review: "Directions to Stone Nest Dojo" and "A Stone Nest Tuesday in June" (2023)

Zartaar Lit: "Between the Image and the Ashes" and "Master to Monks" (2025)

Zest of the Lemon: "Lightenment" (2025)

PROEM

LEAVING THE ABBOT BEHIND

—for Dana Wilde, after Du Fu

The shoreless river flows east and west
but one cuckoo monk has flown to Stone Nest.
This complicated life floats and drifts:
when will it reach its destination?

The second aging abbot, soaked in words not wine,
fled the urban temple to dry out here.
Still bothered by earthly cares, he bows
to his master in the haggard mirror.

Back then we stood, bamboo in bleeding hand;
then lavender bloomed at Napoleon and
a hurricane swept us like clouds and water adrift
to dissolve the dogmas of north and south.

I meet my old friend in a foreign landscape;
newly happy, unburden my heart to him.
The sky is vast, peakless the mountain pass.
Yet fear and desire taunt me still.

A Tennessee wind now billows our robes;
I'm ready to sink like the setting sun.
The great vehicle sputters, stalls, needs work.
Returning birds fold threadbare wings and perch.

The places where we used to meet
nettles have made impassable.
We look each other over and agree:
we still must do what needs to be done.

PEAKLESS MOUNTAIN

There it was, word for word,
The poem that took the place of a mountain.

—Wallace Stevens

FORMLESS MERIT

Here on the mountain we may not be closer to God
but we're closer to the ancient Chinese poets
who chose to be closer to nature and themselves.

Here we can have a conversation without the noise
of academic debate and spiritual conquest,
nothing to achieve, no goal and no rewards.

All formless merit seeping from the thirsty springs,
boulders slowly melting under the gentle torture of being
time, together even though we are so far apart in every way.

We are warmed by the oaks not yet cut down for kindling,
drink muscadines not yet crushed into wine,
eat ripe persimmons bursting with juice only in our minds.

DIRECTIONS TO STONE NEST DOJO

Sherwood Road wraps the mountain like a black river.
Trucks make their way upstream, grunting and shifting gears,
carrying Alabama gravel for the roads of rich and poor,
carrying Georgia provisions for the living and the dead.

You'll find Stone Nest turnoff in the crook of a dead man's elbow.
A dark tunnel of tall trees and green rocks leads to us.
Park down by the blasted tree in the circle,
overlooking the meadow where lightning bugs flicker.

In the shadows of great boulders where leaves are thick
black racers wag their faux rattlers, slither, curl, and dance.
A black dog finds one and fences with it, back and forth,
both poised, each playful, careful, quick, askance.

SEMIS CLIMB THE MOUNTAIN ROAD

—after Liu Chih

Each morning these bright green trees filter sunlight.
These buildings built like boulders on the slope

echo far-off groans as semis climb the Sherwood Road.
All those days wasted down below:

high status, six figures, what was all that about?
low status, wage labor, what was all that?

Youth, ambition, illusions of insecurity,
knowledge squandered on chapters of industry,

middle age full of delusions of success,
meaningless titles mere echoes of grandeur.

We have crisscrossed half the continents, you and I.
Enough! Flowers fall, floods come, footsteps fade.

On busyness man is bent;
idleness is heaven-sent.

WIND FLOWS OVER STONE NEST DOJO

—after Huang Tingjian

On the mountain was raised over the course of fifty years
a residence that came to be called the Laughing Place.
I came and renamed it Stone Nest Dojo for a reason.
Boulders the size of houses overhang the house,
shadows the size of my life cloud my horizon.
The wind whistles through the ancient stones:
no need to be a monk to hear it.
No need to wash your ears in the bodhisattva spring.
Just two or three earnest practitioners in the morning
and the sound of the rain outside the open windows is enough.
Everyone's looking for something, nothing, anything at all.
Whatever it is or isn't they will find it here.
We are all monks in the wilderness during flood and famine.
Only the beauty of the mountains to feed on in the end.
Su Shi, Li Bai and even Huang Tingjian have all gone to rest.
When will the likes of them be heard again?
Not fishing, not swimming, we sleep through the day.
Museums wrap masterpieces with dragons' tails.
How can we help but be caught up in this life
when boats ferry our friends in the ten directions?

INSINUATIONS OF WINTER

Signs of autumn, unmistakable, small
random fires, ignited embers, abruptly
flutter down from the forest canopy
to roll out winter's red carpet of sumac and maple.

Palisades, unbreakable, of Chinese
silver grass in all directions wave
bright pennants and bow as if to pray
for mercy from the coming freeze on bended knees.

Deer appear, ears alert to every footfall,
aware that they're in season, to be culled
as parasites. Smaller prey are not lulled;
red voles start at leaflike shadows cast from hawks overhead.

In closets we dig for gloves and lined wool
barn coats like cassocks that need resewing;
sleep longer now and more soundly knowing
our days, though growing darker, will soon be bright with
                                            snowfall.

DOG DAYS

These long summer months
I sleep all day with Lily and Theo,
black and tan, yin and yang
old and young, male and female,
and me, mister in-between.
(Naps begin soon after dawn
unless it rains and then it's sooner,
lullaby of thunder and pitter-patter
on our shack's tin roof.)
Nothing to do but keep out of the heat
and the world's stupidity. Our tongues
hang to one side like slabs of pink baloney,
ears flop over our eyes like muffs
cooler than Ray-Bans. We make sure
our fluffy heads are lower than our feet
to let the warm blood gravitate,
which helps us not to cogitate too much
while careful, too, not to capsize.
Theo licks the sleep from Lily's eyes
and we all take a moment to lick ourselves
and our heroic but little-used thighs
because we can and in recognition of
old battle scars, dreaming up new
cognomens for our dogged victories.
From time to time we open our eyes
and mouths wide to greet each other
one more time just as the sun is going

down in flames, igniting this evening's
happy-hour cocktail of melatonin
to lull us through another night of rest
and dogeared dreams. Tomorrow we will
wake up to another day of meditative work,
pink palates exposed like washboards,
teeth and tonsils bared,
emitting unhurried
enlightened yawns
for a new dawn.

INSINUATIONS OF SUMMER

Every day now the woods begin to burst
with stippled green at the buds of branches,
the paintbrushes of a pointillist Pan,
triggering another landslide greening—our summer's curse.

These bronze woodscapes like Giacometti nudes
will soon be draped by ten thousand jade fans
and strung with ivies that cloy with poison—
summer's growth strangling the distance and ruining the views.

This summer promises a miracle:
instead of infestations of ladybirds
or carpets of uncoiling copperheads
we'll endure the eclipse of loud cicadas and their reticent shells.

By the billions beaus will be courting belles
(called nymphs) with the silver trill of tymbals
—foreplay approaching ninety-six decibels—
apocalypse of teens sexting, boom boxes in their belly cells.

Their posing will be memorialized
by Dutch doctors with a special amour
for dioramas of deserted armor
stage sets for insect drama by Chekov—very civilized.

HIKING FIERY GIZZARD

—for Leigh, Winter 2023, Tennessee

Two streams converge in a wood of yellow poplar,
by gravity led to some goal as yet unknown:
this carved natural scene—so severe, so serene—
toppling-towering landscape of tacit fallen trees
        and loud waterfalls.

From divergent hidden springs, we have managed, strength
married to strength, through winter's melt and summer's
                                    drought.
Boulders block the path yet never slow the downward
flow that feeds fragrant mosses with fractured moisture
        and faery-filtered light.

Bearded hemlocks, shallow-rooted, heavy-shadowed,
threaten us no more. Your crimson parka leads me,
faithful fool, to plunge headfirst into stony pools
until at last, here, we join forces on the furrowed brow
        of a mountaintop.

Nestled in the naked stone of winter, taking
stock and wisdomless, we anticipate the spring.

WRITTEN FOR THE BACKYARD NATURALIST FROM MAINE

—after Du Fu

We've lived our lives for the most part apart
like the poles of North and South.
Yet this evening we share
the light of one lamp.
Once, for a moment, we were young and sharp:
suddenly dull and gray.
What about old So-and-So? Dead and gone.
Our surprise is no surprise.
How could we have known it would be twenty years
before we met again?
When we parted, your wife was still your bonny sweetheart,
your kids neither married nor buried;
my youngest, not yet conceived.
Unhappy or content, they live their lives,
never asking about our friends.
We don't bother to answer the unquestioned,
they don't bother to fetch the wine.
As the rain falls on the mountain, we chop chives,
mix rice with seeds and dried cherries.
How hard it has been for us to meet in person,
and so we imagine a meal and conversation,
endless drinks yet never a drunken word.
It's your long-lasting friendship that matters.
Tomorrow we'll be parted like the Red Sea;
life will go on, with or without you and me.

IN THE POSTURE OF THE WATER DRAGON

—after Wang Wei

To avoid the stink of incense at the temple,
I wander a few miles along a foggy trail.
No one anywhere on the ancient path between the trees.
A bell rings deep in a dark ravine,
a spring gurgles down a steep rock gulley.
Bright chestnuts chill the prism of slanting light.
At dusk I sit by the calm deserted pool
in the posture of the water dragon.

AS UNATTACHED AS LEAVES IN OCTOBER

—after Bai Juyi

Sometimes I feel like the later Byron,
Woe befall: I've seen it all.

But that's a cynical teenager's call.
In my maturer moments

(call them pantheist sentiments
or the pleasure one feels at simply persisting)

like the old Chinese poets,
I still get a frisson at the coming of fall.

THE SAMADHI OF WORDS

Delusion itself is satori.
   —Kodo Sawaki

Bai Juyi used to beat himself up
for not being able to rid himself
of poetry, the last attachment.

He shouldn't have been so hard on himself:
after all, there is such a thing as
the samadhi of words.

Now, the *satori* of words is a common
phenomenon in the literature of Zen:
an innocent conversation, then: *POP!*

goes the weasel of enlightenment.
Poetry is different. The punchline is not
the point: it's the meditative state that matters.

The journey not the destination
is a threadbare cliche, but each day
must be lived on its own terms, okay.

Samadhi not as a funerary monument,
nor as intense concentration, a high
the opposite of dizziness: *hishiryo.*

Thinking-not-thinking, yes, but the magic
of samadhi is *absorption*, and for me
(and Bai Juyi) what absorbs the mind *is* poetry.

SOMETHING FOR SU TUNGPO

Like a hummingbird suspended above the trumpet blossoms
I have stopped writing poetry
to guzzle it.

Chinese ink this season is most delicious, like dry red wine,
so much black nectar in my throat
I am speechless.

Soon, like a traveler's horse at a waystation eating oats,
I will hear humming in my ears
and write again.

Don't worry about me, hunting season is long—my wing drips
like a clutch of bloodied arrows—
and my proboscis wet.

A STONE NEST TUESDAY IN JUNE

Soft morning rain whispers at the windows,
taps at the rooftops for our attention,
which it had long before it began,
rain's sweet scent a pleasant portent.

All day this soft call to meditation has fallen,
washing weird planarians from their haunts,
fiery salamanders from their lazarus caves;
I lean back and watch clouds fill the valley below.

AFTER HARD RAIN

—after Du Fu

Look around you! Wake up!
The heavens burst wide open; storm clouds now
are dry.

The south wind has migrated
ten thousand miles. This afternoon landscape,
how fine!

Hard rain hasn't hurt the plants
at all. In fact, spears of silver grass are grinning
with new growth.

Redbuds blush with an antic
glow. A dulcimer twangs on a balcony
somewhere.

A pelican clambers into
the sky.

CUSP OF APRIL

last day of March
startled into spring
severe thunderstorms
rattle shoot and branch

lightnings galvanize
japanese maple cotyledons
chinese silvergrass
spears appear

burst of sudden fresh
surprise of leafy blush
it's all happened before
and it's happening again

just like last year at this time
just like in a former life.

PETRICHOR

Bakersfield

Some droughts cause famine
others engender a new hobby

Like xeriscaping or shaming
the neighbors for washing their cars

In the meantime we are reminded
of clean desert smells

New beauties of the *ungreen*
of fishhook cactus and dragon's blood

Purple agave and euphoric firesticks
smokebush and lavender

Our summer skin turns to paper
our hair to dry grass and crushed sage

If we are lucky, if we are blessed
the selfish gods will open a vein

Raising a smokeless cloud of incense
vapor on a hot sidewalk

New smells with new names emerge
like *petrichor*, the scent of rain on dry earth.

POSTCARD: RETURNING FROM ARIZONA IN JUNE

In Sedona
June has all but dried up
bright as sunburnt flesh
crisp as parchment.

Such a shame spring has fled so soon,

I scribble, only to find it
here waiting for me
like honey in a jar
in Tennessee.

ZAZEN AT STONE NEST

Isolated in my hermitage
I almost miss the communion
of men.

Beyond the birdsong outside
the window in the distance
I imagine I hear raised
voices of contention,

then settle back
in the peace of my seclusion
again.

THE TEACHER KEEPS HIS COUNSEL

—after Wang Wei

I am old: I know the value of silence.
The world's much-ado is no longer my problem.

Turning inward, my goal is no goal,
the emptiness of an old forest.

Through shagbark hickories mosquitoes
come to kiss my collarbone; I don't care.

Moon shines bright through high oak
branches; I strum a spiderweb.

I am asked endless open-ended questions:
misguided tribes play war games with real guns.

I CLIMB STONE NEST IN SILENCE

—after Li Yu

I climb Stone Nest in silence,
the moon like a kitchen knife.

Late autumn clarity illuminates
the blasted tree in the drive.

Memories of parting,
dérèglement de tous les sens,

and the psychic savor
of long-gone haunts.

You can almost hear
this crackling moon

in the clarity of frozen air
as it undresses for the day.

BETWEEN THE IMAGE AND THE ASHES

Sitting between the image and the ashes
in the crosshairs of the patriarchy
your six senses empty out and grow calm.
You feel the sizzle of incense, smell the tang of bells,
hear your shadow sit up straight, see the breeze of the fan,
taste the dharma, and know
that all of this is Nothing.

Having ridden the horses of instruction,
having mounted the lions of wrath,
you wield the invisible sword that cuts illusion
forging a path of your own between patriarchs,
cutting down those pious devils left and right,
images and ashes, to become your own
master among the masters.

YES, EMPTINESS

These snowcloud mountains
    struck by a slanting
        sliver of dawn—
            an avalanche
                of silence.

OUT WITH THE OLD

—after Su Shi

Soon we'll say good riddance to the old year
like a snake that slithers into its hole.
Its scaly length is almost all hidden
and no one can keep it from going.
Even if we tie its tail in colorful ribbons,
no matter how we try, we fail.
The kids roughhouse to stay up late,
everyone wide awake with fireworks.
Roosters refuse to call the dawn
and so should all your alarm clocks.
All our candles are wasted away,
all the stars have faded.
This year I fear my time may be up.
Maybe I've run out of luck.
Tonight let's make merry while we can,
while youth still has the upper hand.

THE ZEN MONK TO HIS DESIGNER DOG

I speak metaphorically of course but you have
the eyes of a philosopher with a fluffy face.

There was a time when I would cuddle only cats,
but there was always something missing—
their aloofness, I suppose, but also the hissing,
tarted up in their tuxedos, spats and white cravats.

Sometimes I wonder when I'm speaking to you
if you understand what I'm talking about.
You gaze with such sage curiosity and doubt
as though you get me, or at least would like to.

Then you nip at my knuckles like they're your chew toys
or leap into bed and lave my ears with your velvet tongue,
something I confess I may enjoy too much.
Then we wrestle like a couple of buddha boys.

I speak metaphorically of course, but you have
the eyes of a philosopher with a fluffy face.

STILL LIFES EVERYWHERE

I don't want to be out of this world, I want
to be absolutely in it, all of the time.
  —Lucian Freud

If you think about it but not too much
there are still lifes everywhere
everywhere there is life it is still.

If you don't think about it too much
but observe, quietly, without fanfare
there and there and there is life, still.

There is the dog on the carpet in front of the window
its paws on your feet, positioned just so as though
he knows he is being immortalized in paint or photo

in art or in your heart.
But first you must be still yourself
still enough to be alive to what is still life.

CEMENT BUDDHA

Outside Point Barre in St. Landry Parish
in a weathered notch of the Bible Belt,
the roadside cement statuary beckons
like a graveyard of petrified angels and animals.
Rampant bear, delicate deer, and astonished dolphin
surround a pair of St. Francis twins, while an array
of stiff Marys in white and skyblue latex paint stand
like pawns instead of the Queen of Heaven. Saints here
sell, though they seem fewer as we head north and
enter the twi-faith zone between swamp and prairie
Catholics and born-again hill-pine evangelicals.

With one eye always peeled for Buddhas,
oddly enough I find one here. Fat, not laughing
but with a patient grin, ears drooping to his
waist like Granny's dewlaps. The car is packed
full of books, mid-move, so I plant him on the floorboard
between my legs, his cueball head a third knee,
where he can't see the road ahead—or me.
The old woman who collects the cash insists
that the Hindu clan who run the motel next door
down Hwy 55 are like family when she takes me aside
and, crossing herself, sells him to me.

THE SHOCK OF RECOGNITION

A book is a mirror: if an ape looks into it
an apostle is unlikely to look out.
            —Georg Christoph Lichtenberg

When we come face to face with our real self
(the one we could never think up)
it won't be in a window or mirror.

Will we recognize our glass reflection?
This blank stare of a blank slate
comes from nowhere and goes nowhere.

Like Dōgen's enlightened scarecrow
(*How clueless! How useful!*)
how like a manikin in monastic robes.

It won't be what we envisioned, no sage
(more like a madman or moron)
when we come self to self with our real face.

NIGHTTIME THOUGHTS ON THE MOUNTAIN

—after Du Fu

A soft wind combs the tall grass;
a white oak pierces the Tennessee sky;

Constellations drip silver rain on the meadow;
the moon rises over the domain's plateau.

Every song I've written remains unsung:
aging poets like me should shut up and listen.

Yet I keep squawking, a mockingbird
stranded between shoveled earth and bright sky.

OLD POETS, OLD FROGS

Last night the loud frog leapt
into the illusion of a lily
and slipped on the ice.

Li Po embraced the moon
in the lake and drowned.

Old frogs can still skim like a stone
or a song's echo
when they've had too much to drink.

Old poets, when they've had too much
to think, sink like a stone.

FROM STONE NEST TO THE SUNFLOWERS

After heavy rain, the trail is soft and dark.
Fresh tracks of mythical wildlife we never
manage to see. A muddy ford. A fallen tree.
My bad attitude, your trick knee. Those don't
stop us. We hike the path we've beaten
from Stone Nest to the Sunflowers.

No chanterelle but other fans unfold:
red-capped, spotted, and golden-gilled,
some nourishing, some lethal, a colorful few
offering visions. We pass them all by
unsure of the differences between
these spontaneous beauties and poison beasts.

Trilliums droop near summer's end
like faded beach umbrellas. Ivies extend
their poison fingers everywhere
from the foot of trees to their canopies.

Insects greet and greedily feed on us,
mosquitoes, invisible spiders, chiggers,
and deer flies with razor lips.
We are the forest's food-trucks.

Having hiked from Stone Nest to the Sunflowers,
we kiss, make up without shame or blame,
turn, and retrace our steps,
from the Sunflowers back to Stone Nest.
The trail gets harder every day, and darker,
but this is how trails are traced to last.

THE PAST IS NOT PAST IN SEWANEE, TENNESSEE

—after Huang Tingjian

Here on the mountain in all directions graveyards
abound. Grief echoes and fog glows: angels and ghosts
of Confederate orphans. Moonshine tears are shed
and dons don the scarlet and ermine of religion.

As the sun sets, foxes lope past the library
to return to their dens; young couples couple on
tombstones. While you have it, drink deeply of your wine.
History is a memory unworthy of honest men.

DEEP SPRING RAIN HAS PASSED

—after Ouyang Xiu

Deep spring rain
has passed.

Tall grasses
grow like girls.

Chaos of butterflies,
cacophony of bees.

The clear day spurs
the world to beauty.

RETURNING TO LIVE IN THE SOUTH

—after Tao Qian

When I was young, I disdained the simple pleasures,
though my deepest love was always wooded mountains:
Big Bear, Big Sur, the Cascades and Carpathians.
I fell for the texture of big and bigger cities;
thus I wandered for more than fifty years.
A songbird travels till it finds its true nest.
A fish takes freely to the lake where it spawned.
A dog can locate its ancestors' scent.

The Welsh have a saying, *Dod yn ôl at fy nghoed*
I return to my trees, to balance, to my senses.
I've returned to a South where I'd never been,
two dozen acres of woodland and boulders,
half a dozen rooms sprawled on a Cumberland brow.
Shade from white oaks, hemlocks, and shagbark hickories;
persimmons drop their fruit in late autumn, I'm told.
Up the road lies a college, a library for the learned.

Here, coyotes bark in the distance at night.
Frogs croak baritone to the recent rain.
I write poetry in echo out of key.
Promiscuous cowbirds and woodpeckers never rest.
The dust of the world stops at my door.
These rooms are modest and mostly vacant.
I'd be happy to end my life here where I'm free,
set upright in myself again—before it's too late.

THE VIEW FROM MY WINDOW

—after Wang Wei

A hawk soars into the distance
where mountain slopes meet
around about the Alabama border
and autumn's fires dance.

The Cumberland Plateau surrounds us
like a fulldome cinema:
a melancholy scenario
that knows no horizon.

MINDFULNESS

Like a dog

finding just the right
place to place
his toys his balls his bone

a fragrant log

a good dog
he always considers
and considers and considers

before he commits.

OLD STONES, NEW BUDDHAS

old stones grizzled with lichen
hoary with moss
solid stolid and mountain still

new monks freshly robed and shaved
trembling with insight
spring from Stone Nest on black wings

SHORELESS RIVER

*It was passing a boundary, floating without a head
And naked, or almost so, into the grotesque...*

—Wallace Stevens

SHORELESS RIVER

Bywater, New Orleans

I walked to the river with some students today
to look at ourselves without mirrors

Fog lay thick on the far bank
tall buildings afloat

Pages of our notebooks flutter
in no breeze, pens poised

Tugboats, noses in the air like dogs
paddle upstream south to the Gulf

Here, where bodies of weather and water meet
the rains never come quietly.

LIGHTENMENT

The light that races in the early morning
across the beadboard panels

Light that astonishes
Light that pinpoints our focus

The waterfall light on the wall
from the melting windows

The light in animal eyes

Light that fades a signature
in a work of art

Light that makes us lose our minds
Light we forget to listen to

Humid light that blurs the distinction
between our skin and chaos

Reflected light that binds and blinds

Light that makes us lose our focus
Light that flashes from total blackness

Crisp winter light that washes the sky
from cerulean to cyan to periwinkle blue

Inner light that brightens the body

The dying light burning up the horizon

The light that lightens our load

Light that lights the light.

GIACOMETTI FOREST

In every work of art the subject is primordial.
—Alberto Giacometti

I wonder: why bray
about heaven-on-earth
when this earth is already
better than any heaven
we might imagine?
For example:

The stillness
when these
winter trees
are stripped
and whittled
into bronze
Giacomettis
swaying in place
on thick leafy carpets
silent with forest fog
an empty museum.

Fog that comes down from the cold
shoulder of ridgetops.
Fog that comes up from the warm
bosom of black soil.
Fog that hides in the cold
crotch of hidden coves.
Fog that emerges from the warm
throat of the valley.
Fog that settles at the cold
foot of a neglected trail.
Fog that rests in the warm
bed of the somnolent meadow.
Fog that romances all it embraces
from decrepit chapels to hidden hollows.

These fogs clothe us
in canopies
of stillness,
like those naked
Giacometti refugees
attenuated,
slow-dancing in place
in profile
in the round
on patinated pedestals
of stone-cold fear and
rapt with thermal
earth-desire.

We
ourselves
are refugees
from the so-called
civilized:
winter trees
stripped,
temporarily
enfeebled,
whittled
into living
Giacomettis,
powerless to resist
the seasonal rhythm.
We sway
with them and sometimes
weep at the beauty
of unacknowledged beauty.

IN THE ART WORLD

... as we all know from arithmetic lessons,
two into three won't go.
    —Martin Gayford

Here in the art world everything
exists in two dimensions

Dérèglement de tous les sens
moral and sensual, logic and humor

Though we yearn for flesh and blood to emerge
from these plays of shadow lights, just like that

Just like Pygmalion erupting warm and naked
from a three-tiered birthday cake

Mockingbird caged in its blood-matte background
cartoon dog cutout with its goofy black-and-white grin

Three-dimensional figures are delusional: Tantalus
as *Articulated Man Dancing with a Pear*

Never will he drink from that *Liquore Galliano*
commemorative pitcher of liquid gold

Even the mantle where these works are propped
is not a mantle but a mask, a mirror, a sign:

NO PARKING CAR STOP
clearly a koan.

SATORI

don't get a swelled head
even the full moon
lasts only one night
        —Sengai at 87 on satori

You pay attention:

In the slow gloaming
a sudden burst of bats
of this way and thats
glanced and gone
a puff of air
a pair of
zigzagging shadows
glimpses caught like mosquitoes midflight
a glinting flutter of eyelids
at the edge of the wild
reflected light
halfmoonlight
artificial light
dying light
naturally
unconsciously
spontaneously
tossed back to you
(gloomlight!)
like a ball in your court
from your own torch

Now what do you do?

DARUMA GETS HIS EARS CLEANED

Even the wisest among us is
no saint, all numskulls, no
exception.

Whether we can hear the music of suffering
or not
whether we've spent nine years banging our eyes
against the wall of a made-up cave
or not
whether our arms fall from our sides
or our legs from our hip sockets
or not
whether tea leaves spring up when our eyelids drop off
or coffee beans hang like tears from our lashes
or not
whether our tongues like flags are idle or flapping
or not
whether our students cut off their hands for us
sew us okesas with nine bands
or not
whether we arise from our own emptiness enlightened
or not
whether our throats are clogged with chant
or (more likely) cant
or not

none of us is exempt.

NO LONGER DRUNK ON THE ROAD AT NIGHT

—after Li Yu

Last night wind and rain danced frantic till dawn.
Window curtains clapped for their mournful song.
The power went out and the clocks all stopped.
I got up and sat for a while but could not sit for long.

When my daughter was a baby, she loved to sing along:
Row row row your boat, life's a butter dream.
How like a storm are our short lives, flooded with forgetting,
ashes and gold nuggets gushing down gutters in a stream.

I used to think I should spend more time drunk on the road
    at night
so that I might live, so that I might think I continued to live.
But now the memory of a kid's misprision
hits me like a Blakean vision.

I want to go back and row a boat over butter;
I want to go back and do it all over—but better.

DRINKING WINE AT STONE NEST

—after Tao Qian

I have settled here above the human hustle
where I hear very little of machines
and machinations.

How did you do it, you may ask.
An estranged heart will find its proper place—
eventually.

I plant juniper and rhododendron, lambs' ears and mint,
gaze out on the southern hills toward Alabama
and beyond.

The mountain air tastes luxurious night and day,
birds flock together, slant in flight and seem to frolic,
angry or at play.

I sense that all this has a deeper meaning:
I search for the words in the bottom of my glass
but find only my reflection.

A KAYAK ON BAYOU ST. JOHN AT JAZZ FEST

—*after Ouyang Xiu*

A kayak with orange oars. Bayou St. John's
muddy water gently stagnates

Swampgrass along the banks
faint saxophones follow us everywhere

No wind ripples the glassy surface
no canoes pass us by. We sip cold beer from koozies

Tiny movements startle the wildlife
turtles and alligator snouts break the mirror glaze.

SUNDAY PARTY BOAT, BAYOU ST. JOHN

—after Ouyang Xiu

A bright boat full of beer and beer drinkers
plangent tenor horns and soothing bass strings

Foaming go-cups everywhere
floating on the gentle stream, the SS *Dead Drunk*

See how the clouds slide under the boat
how the dirty water reflects the blue sky

Look up, look down, look all around
here on the bayou, just another sort of heaven.

IDLENESS (NESTING)

—after Li Yu

Once we had a doorbell.
We had it disconnected.
Who wants strangers traipsing mud and dust in?
All those boots and bloody bootstraps.

It's summertime at last.
You can hear the Harleys on the road below.
My wife is reading Homer.
She asks me about some mythological swine.

My daughter wants a sip of wine
and drains the glass before I can snatch it back.
Is there anything better than a place in the country
with a private trail among the trees?

THE BUDDHA IN THE BUSHES

Three cheers for the poetry of subjectivity—
but I have to admit that nowadays my poetry
is all outside of me and has been ever since
my daughter came down on this mortal scene
trailing clouds of innocence
and otherworldly experience.

Here's what I mean:

In the garden by the pool one day
where she is swimming with her snakes,
I am trying to create a clearing poolside
when I slice my wrist with a bamboo blade
(not suicidal, just a fool not paying
attention to what I was doing).

She slips out of the water dripping
like some celestial otter to the rescue.
I watch in awe as she calmly patches me up
with Gorilla Glue. Ignoring the blood,
she is all business applying
the soggy blue Elmo and Ernie bandaid
with expert fingers before returning
to her friends, all green and golden, like whips
awaiting her impatiently in the clear blue water.
They always come to her when she calls,
and now they call to her until
she dives back in to be with them.

Was it me who taught her to swim like that?
I seem to recall her throaty laughter,
the joy of the conqueror,
the first time she swam across by herself
before she befriended her serpentine pals.

Now she climbs out, pointing to the clearing
among the bamboo spears and saw palmettos
and says with conviction:
The Buddha statue will go there—in the bushes:
it will help you swim because you do zazen.
Then she rejoins her slithery friends.

THE HERMIT PUTS OUT A MISSION STATEMENT

So sense exceeds all metaphor.
        —Wallace Stevens, "Bouquet of Roses in Sunlight"

I am no shaman or prophet but
as a priest of an unpopular religion I
have come to the mountaintop to
practice with two or three acolytes what
passes in these latter days for
magic: embracing
the everyday the
miraculous ordinary.

I have no answers for truth seekers
only a few tools and permission to dig deep and
travel wide in the capacious
realms where no parents or teachers have
ventured and no preachers dare spread
their wings because here
sacred and profane merge in the
clear air of the real.

Some prefer the art of the caves of
the Cumberland Plateau where the twilit gods of the
underworld flit with the painted
bats and birds below, but I am one of
those old birds who nest in the stones
on high where the bluffs are
carved with lichened images that
can't be named or tamed.

MASTER TO MONKS

I can't teach you anything!
Everything must come through your own efforts.
You didn't know it would be this difficult, did you?
You thought you would munch tasteless vegan meals;
instead you were served whisky and raw meat.
Now you are on your own. Now you know you always were.
Don't wait for me to die. Kill me now! You can try.
Some of you know this already. Some never will. Some know why.
The gentle temple down the road says of our mountain monastery
that we throw cubs off the cliff to see if they'll survive.
    Ha! It's true.
They will catch you and feed you pale piss and pablum,
    don't worry.
Some of you have been tossed rudely from the nest.
Some tried to fly too soon and fell.
Too many have broken their wings on the rocks.
A few fell between the cracks and are plummeting still.
A few of you will manage to fly in spite of me.
This does not mean you can dispense with me.
On the contrary, I am here to affirm your flight
(the I who am not I).
Even when I am silent or not around
I will always be air to your gravity
and the rock that blocks the summit of the steep path.

THE MAN IN THE BLUE WHEELCHAIR

It must be this rhapsody or none,
The rhapsody of things as they are.
        —Wallace Stevens, "The Man With the Blue Guitar"

The old man bent over in his wheelchair
he was a sage of sorts. Naked

he held a bottle of cheap pinot noir
to his breast like a suckled choir

Asleep, he did not snuffle, snore or snort
all complaints now in the past

Once upon a time he taught us all
to see things as they are:

Unobstructed mind is a mirror
where clouds can never disturb the eye

Once awakened he stared down the room
at the full-length mirror, too blind to see

Himself reflected there. He was aware
only that it was an open door into

Another room, another reality
Shut that door, he demanded

(*It's only a mirror,* came the answer)
Shut it anyway, he commanded

The cat doesn't know that and
She will get out, so shut it!

The cat in the end did not make her escape
but the old man did. It's possible

He passed through his reflection. Now
when I catch a glimpse of myself

In a mirror, startled, I wonder:
when will it be my turn

To pass through all this illusion
into the rhapsody of things as they are.

REMEMBERING REIBIN

—after Su Shi

This life of ours, what is it?
A Mardi Gras parade of cuckoo Zen monks
smoking hash on the banks of a shoreless river,
where they flick their ashes
and drift away, some east, some west.

Well, the old monk is no more.
An urn was carved for him—out of bamboo of course.

Inside the broken walls of the Camp Street temple
you can no longer hear the echo of the kusen he spoke.
There's nothing to show we were ever there.
The way was long. We were all exhausted.
Just time's betrayal, like a broken down van.

STILL MOURNING MY LATE ZEN MASTER

—after Meng Haoran

I often yearn to kick back on a hilltop:
instead I have to hustle for donations.

I never thought I'd leave the Gulf,
those dizzying expanses of the horizontal.

Yet now I keep my teacher deep in a forest,
his ashes in a golden bamboo urn.

Visions flatten what once was vertical;
my lofty ideals melt away year by year,

Suns don't set and cold winds disappear.
Cicadas cry for me and then cry for me.

THE OLD BIRD

Prepare for the day
when you no longer need to prepare
your resume

Attending my old teacher
for twenty-some-odd years . . .

In his prime his profile
the stone beak of a predatory hawk.

His eyes the icepick gaze
of ice-blue ice.

In his final days the glaze
began to melt.

His silhouette feathered into softness so
that he became almost human.

Until the day he curled into a fetal
enso of flesh.

He lay that morning on his deathbed,
an egg in a stone nest.

And although we knew he had flown,
we chanted the emptiness sutra for him.

Now suddenly it's I who am old,
perched here on this clifftop aerie,

Tired, cold, empty, alone,
yet not yet ready to rest.

THERE'S SOMETHING ABOUT BAMBOO

Robert Livingston Roshi (1933–2021)

There's something about spun bamboo
—T-shirts and winding sheets, for example—
that's like mint on the skin.

One you slip on first thing in the morning,
the other you slip into in the end.

I used to think texture was the be-all and end-all
and I'm beginning to think so again.

Here and now. My teacher was a master
of many things, not of himself perhaps,

but he was never so much himself as in his garden
even more than when he was teaching Zen.

Above all he was a master of bamboo—
of its majestic height and its tensile strength

and how its roots burrow under earth's skin
without regard for property or propriety,

not unlike him, he himself, who still speaks
of the wonders of bamboo to me and now to you,

though his ashes rest in this
carved cubicle of an urn of minty grass.

TO THE ASHES OF MY MASTER ON THE ALTAR

Taikaku Reibin Daiosho

1

He was never mundane, no one was ever
less Prufrock than he.

Yet now I measure out his life in coffeespoons
for the devoted who ask.

His name was Spiritual Vivacity
a Living Stone

A dragon's voice in the dojo, a handful of dust—
he marked us.

His legacy, after all, this Great Palace of meat sacks
sitting for a moment like mountains, here and now, this morning.

As he did for decades, drinking the oceans of east and west
we love and die alone.

On this mountain, in this temple, like a jar in Tennessee
the slovenly wilderness all around.

2

As he grew old, he never wore the bottoms of his trousers rolled—
in the end he never wore anything at all

Shin jin datsu raku, throwing off body and mind, and even Zen
like so many dregs for the compost heap

Throwing out mad resident monks, throwing cubs
off the cliff to see if they'd survive.

Now I measure out his teaching in small doses like poison
for the devoted who don't know what to ask.

To enrich their new soil with only the essential minerals
of his eternal childishness,

His spontaneity, his wisdom, his poetic emptiness
the direct mind, the effortless skill, the real thing

All the leftover sarira of his delusions and earthly delights
that come to dust like the rest of us.

Each ash of his body-mind in its bamboo urn
a spark of satori to light the fire in our hair

Each ash of us sitting up like a samurai in zazen
head pressing the sky.

ANXIETY

Our shelves are full of books
we don't read

The fridge is full of fruit
we won't eat

Our veins are full of blood
we can't feel

The fireplace is full of wood
that doesn't burn

Our sleep is full of dreams
we don't dare

The world is full of fear
we can't hear

Our bank account is full of money
we won't spend

The hives are full of honey
we can't share

The meadow is full of turkey vultures
we don't fear

Our mailbox is full of mail
we don't open

The world is full of hatred
we can't bear

Our guns are full of bullets
we refuse to fire

Time is full of opportunities
we don't take advantage of

Our hearts are full of love
we die of.

SUNYATA

Jerry Peterson (1952–2007)

Today I read how you sat in your Gretna law office
on Monday and held a 9mm to your head.

With what version of emptiness were you
infatuated? What were you aiming at?

Having interrogated your brain to the edge
of an abyss, having heard *l'appel du vide*,

In the forest of suicides questions are left
hanging. Seppuku, jumper, or accidental OD?

What was it Buckminster Fuller did *not* say?
the *method* is the message.

There's no recall from the void, no appeal
once you pull the trigger.

All night I couldn't sleep; all day I couldn't
convince myself of the wisdom to weep.

With a bottle of bourbon on the porch swing I sit
and witness the bag of heaven burst

With chest-pounding thunder and lightning,
gavels of the gods in the distance.

I am left without judgment mid-sentence
in the twilight of an ambiguous reprieve.

Let the entire cosmos mourn, I raise my glass
to the unbiased beauty of this violent storm.

MI FU BOWING TO THE STONE

They say he was mad. Before visiting
his flesh and blood he would pay his respects
by bowing to his adopted elder
brother in the garden: a great huddled
boulder of gray weathered stone.

People round here are polite. When I came
to the mountain and changed the grass hut's name
from The Laughing Place to Stone Nest Dojo,
no one minded, they laughed, as if I were
another old Madman Mi.

We sit together, Mi and I, and share our art,
sketching the fog with brushes heavy with fog.

CACTI IN THE CABIN WINDOW

We place these cacti in the cabin window,
our bright new winter crushes, kept fresh
and zaftig inside under glass.

Outside in the garden fall's flashy flowers fade,
mere guests of the hour, waste away, expire,
queued up for their annual checkout.

These prickly new pets somehow disarm us,
charm us with their shapely sincerity,
lilliputian thimbles, bunny ears, urchins

impervious to any temporary lack
or our indifference. Nothing personal.
These potted dual-sexpots

store summer's fire inside their waxen skin,
grow garish lumps like gush tumors, rare
blossoms not for display in civilized vases.

Some so cute they seem to have faces, comic
or dour, sprouting phallic spires and white glochid
wires from a wart on a wen on a witch's chin.

We've become devotees of such weird succulence
with fearless fingers knowing just how to stroke
a fine head of spines, touchy as alien porcupines.

Like right now: basking in the magnifying
glass, our green and fuzzy flora, defiant,
independent, keen, needles sparkling in sunlight.

A priceless treasure on any other planet,
      O the brash beauty of thee
      and thy multiform deformity!

Unlike so many spring and summer loves
who withered under my prisms,
I couldn't kill you if I tried.

IDLE IN THE STUDY, WINTER, WITH DOGS

Sitting in the new study, taking in the view
level with the planed horizon of the Cumberland
Plateau, I wonder how it would be to entertain here.

To sit with old friends and family and new, and take in
the view together. In silence. But when they arrive
they talk too loud and look longingly only at their phones.

Thanksgiving sunlight yearns to stroke my granddaughter's
Pre-Raphaelite hair. How it enwraps her shoulders
like a golden baby blanket or a shroud for her shyness!

No, better to sit with old ghosts, friendly visitations,
holograms who never bellyache about the infestation
of Asian lady beetles or spend all day texting distant besties.

That same sunlight now collapses on the threshold
like a bright vampire sprawled on the black slate tile, waiting
to be invited in. Or some evanescent Edinburgh memory,

warm and sultry in the wintery light. The books behind me
in the shelves whisper our old secrets, bits of wisdom, travels
to places we've been in our minds. Only the dogs

understand, one splayed in my leather reading chair,
the other on his back, head on my lap. Only they
can be still and unworried about all that remains undone.

CARAPACES

1

Just before our daughter moved away to grad school
she and I were outside looking at the stars and marveling
at the carapace of space.
                          A rustling in the bushes
startled me. She began to laugh and laugh at me, knowing
better than I the landscape and wildlife in these parts
and what was coming.
                          A convoy of armadillos
trooped right between us as though we were invisible
(or they were blind), waddling with supreme confidence
each in its nine-banded carapace
                          and the cloak of a summer night.
Three of them: a parent, I presume, and its offspring,
to judge by the protocol they followed,
single file by size, large to small.
                          What focused insouciance!
The next day we packed up and caravaned to St. Louis,
two cars and her belongings under the orange and
silver-gray carapace of a UHaul trailer.

2

It has been the summer of death and beauty. Old friends
have passed away. Or, yes, as we say of our appliances,
they *died*, malfunctioned, ran out of gas, went . . . offline.
                          The machine that hosted the ghost: kaput.
Unlike our automobiles, cell phones and computers, never to be
restored, recharged, or reformatted. One by one, they've
                          stopped working:
a grade-school pal, an elder brother, a suicide,
                          a friend too seldom met.

3

Back from St. Louis, I hike the trail behind the house
and come across the carcass of an armadillo
lying on its side. Recently deceased,
                    unless it's napping.
I nudge it with the toe of my boot to see if it might be
woken if not revived. But no, even though it has not begun
the quick process of summer decomposition,
                    it isn't coming back.
I assume it is one from the convoy the other night,
I assume it is the parent as would only be right
and leave it there for the coyotes, foxes, and raccoons
                    to recycle overnight.
It doesn't take long. In a few days, I hike the trail again,
and there it is, where I left it, hollowed out and clean
as a desert-bleached skull:
                    an empty, whitened carapace.

4

Duly noted: the nine-banded armadillo's carapace
(or osteoderm) protects it from predators
                    (who prize its delicate flesh).

Duly noted: the nine-paneled kesa, the Zen monastic's robe
(or okesa), is for teachers who are authorized
                    to ordain new monks on the Way.

5

My daughter, by the way, started grad school today.
Considering the fragility of carapaces,
I worry about her, but she says
                    O Dad I'm doing fine.

THE DEATH OF TWO POSSUMS

We can't help it: we are meaning-making machines.

On her way home at the dangerous bend
In the road she hit a possum, or rather
This possum slunk under her wheels, *thunk thunk*, the end.

Moments later she texted her boyfriend
Who, also on his way home, glanced at his phone:
Thus another possum (what are the chances?) met its end.

This is where the rubber meets the rodent
He thought, *har har*, then quickly had to amend
His hard-hearted pun because we all know a possum isn't

Some rotund rat but a marsupial.
So begins a conundrum: random events?
Or some insane karmic convergence of the twain?

Even the death of two possums invites
Speculations on free will and theodicy:
No matter how deft our interpretation, it doesn't make it right.

When coincidence meets what is destined
Head on like two arrows meeting, then
As everyone knows, the end is important in all things.

IF WE WIN THE LOTTERY OR ARE REINCARNATED WHICH AMOUNTS TO THE SAME THING

will we make the same mistakes we made
this time around or new ones not based on
early poverty and midlife budgets and old-age
retirement fixed-income funds because we had
frustrated dreams of extraordinary lives
that never came to fruition but descended
into a dim hope of mere dignity
fed on the scraps of social security?
Things change; they always stay the same.
If that's true of the next life, how will we know
since we won't be allowed to take our memories
with us across that rebirthday border like refugees
without papers from our previous lives, but must pledge
to spend our new money like old souls without a care
in the world, much less a family tree
with complete allegiance to this new country
that is not for the young or the old either? The flow chart
of our money and our memories will be erased and all
our friends will become strangers and all our strangers
will become friends—at least they will pretend to be
one or the other or both. All our renewable charitable
contributions will be sent to the old addresses, charged
on the old card, only to be neglected, rejected, denied.
What then? Death and taxes will remain the same
if not loom larger as restraints on our ability to live out
our unlimited ambitions by spending our unearned
money and giving vast pots of invisible gold to charities
with or without our names engraved on lintels
of the institutions we once envied and wanted to emulate
before we die again, go broke again, are put on
the endangered species list again, or simply go extinct.

RIDING AND WRITING IN CIRCLES

They say Buddhist altars should face the east.
My writing desk also faces east but sometimes
the light of the rising sun is blinding.

Back in the day, they say, Zen masters
would pass along the robe and bowl.
Mine passed along this desk.

Covered in old Spanish leather
weathered as an oxblood boot and smooth
as the stone floor of a cathedral,

this old desk is the ox I'm still learning
to ride in circles like the ensos stamped
in wine stains on its hide.

WHAT HANGS IN THE BALANCE

It's winter again and I still
haven't finished painting
the house as I said I would.

I still need to fix that chainsaw,
order a new blade because
the old one's warped.

That's the least of our worries.

Other things got done though:
the garden path is fully pebbled
and weeds no longer choke it.

And thanks to the plumber
the pipes no longer back up
and all things septic flow to the tank.

And so much more.

Firewood is stacked
in stately ricks by the door
ready to keep us cozy till March.

We learned how to use
the pizza oven from Iceland,
an Xmas gift from years ago.

Yet something always remains.

Our mailbox, for example, still leans
and sags and hangs its head from the post
in a precariously symbolic stance.

And whatever it is that is coming our way
in the new year
hangs in the balance.

COLLECTING THE MAIL

When I walk the rise of the driveway to the road
to collect the mail

I take a long look around at the lonely woods
and stop in wonder

Seventy years of stress and striving, what the hell
now have come to this

It's easy not to feel worthy of this earthly
almost-paradise

Like the thrill of an old gambler's one last lucky
shake and toss of dice

A few checks, address changes, cards of condolence—
not a single bill.

BODILY ORIGAMI

—after a poem by Dōgen comparing bowing
to a crane folding up into itself,
or hiding within its own form.

Map of my life
my karma my body
folds up into itself,
creases never
the same way twice,
disintegrates at the
edges, takes me
       still
where I need to go
on paper wings.

I look forward to
throwing this old map
away though, which
once used, will never be
suitable for framing
not even in a shadow
       box
for my widow
to shadowbox with.

The well-thumbed
topography of memory
(a thousand creases
mapped in the brain)
       alone
is worth keeping
keeping it close
keeping it by heart
like marshland littered
with a thousand cranes.

THE CHANGING LIGHT AT STONE NEST

Much of this reminds me of The Third Policeman
absurd gobbledegook but funny if you follow
　　　—from my notes in the margin of James Merrill's epic

Bodhidharma was a bit of a zealot, you have to admit
delving into Plato's cave for nine years
exploring the light in the shadows

Form is a kind of interview (colloquy)
expanding into seminar (theatre)
inviting spirits to indulge in soliloquy

Those legends about the black monk cutting off his eyelids
green tea sprouting from the earth where they fell
arms and legs dropping off like body and mind, well...

How to verify the inspiration of the word
the experimental or even accidental
coincidences of autobiography and culture

Here at Stone Nest we do things with a difference
looking out on the mountaintop at the changing light
in all its quiet magnificence

Nothing is ever settled in such questions
everything in the end is still up for grabs
certainty is sought and then discarded

Each season brings its palette of colors
each week its cast of characters
each moment its intensity

Allowed to filter away in doubt
through gateless gates of ivory and horn
then taken up again

No need to apply to the Sisters of St Mary or
Rotary to pray for us, nor to the arcana of the Tarot
to tell us what we already know we don't know

Like Penelope weaving and unweaving
meaning in the masks of Mirabell, yes yes and no
the light converses, spars with shadow

Does God think and plan like a Victorian novelist?
we sit on the floorboards, yes yes
but who is inscribing/inspiring all this?

Amid the changing light and the calligraphy of scent
making use of the dream's multipurpose props and sets
glimpsed like spirits adrift on the air

The drama (or is it dharma?) unfolds like an origami bible
and ends on a doubtful
almost shamefaced note . . .

WHAT THERE IS LEFT TO DO

Ses purs ongles très hauts dédiant leur onyx . . .
        —Mallarmé

Now that the hand has come full circle
rounding out what could not be rounded out

In time, the heart begins to accept the flaws
in the design. Along the edge of the bed's horizon

The gloss of a fingernail is pointing out
in the West the long-since burnt-out angle

Of the setting sun, its beautiful obsolescence
the way a knuckle stiffens to the lost

Incense of adolescence, an arthritic
instrument measuring absence, time's exalted

Abstinence, that dubious distinction won with ease
the middle-aged man in traffic whirling his arms

In alarm. What is there left to do?
get up and dress for success though you

No longer need it? Try not to recall the missed
rendezvous, the diminishing risk

Or your own heroic future receding
as you advance? After all, you know all this

With digital exactness, the precise
number of your failures to the fraction

Of a second chance, for you never had much luck
at dice or dire predictions. Let it suffice

That you have outlasted the past. In time
the heart begins to accept the flaws in the design.

BEYOND THE BEYOND

We dwell in the texture of the everyday
smelling the coffee, the flowers, the dew

We wake up screwed, in a bad mood
going through the day wanting to be wooed

We go to bed hoping to sleep seven hours
dreaming of putting out fairytale fires

We dream of swimming the Hellespont .
breathing dry sage and mountain tea

We feed on the flesh of the living and the dead
trusting our bellies instead of the beyond

We sing silent songs of premature grieving
chanting monotonous threats of true-believing

We open our hands to let go what we love
and waking up, go beyond the beyond.

SEVENTY-THREE

I knew my time
was running low
weeks ago

when the leaves
of the little Japanese maple
lost their blush

and reddish glow
and curled into sere
arthritic claws

like mine
clutched in the hearty winter
handshake that bestows

the deathgrip
of eternal friendship.

A BAT IN THE PANTRY

A life hidden in seclusion is like what?
   —Bai Juyi

No warning
just a soft flutter that skims /
the top of your head
like a plump putto / not quite
touching down and even softer /
swooshes then darting
this direction and / that
into the too-bright light
rushing to / find its way
out the door into fading / dark
of first morning blush

But at least it / didn't land
like a horrible webbed hand /
in imitation of a human hat / some
misshapen mammalian beret
or / kite-like yarmulke clinging
like a pat / on the head
from a pedophile priest as /
creepy and reassuring
as corrupt / religion can be
as soothing as a / nightshade cap
or an angelic evasion / of the truth

We are no longer scared of / such
surprises that no longer surprise / but
you never know what's next / ? ? ? / bull
frogs with long tongues in the toilet / men
with long guns in the aftermath / stealthy
copperheads in the rocks / healthy wolf
spiders scaling bedroom walls / and now

these indigent bats lost and down / on
their luck demanding their squatter's rights /
indignant in furry flight after hanging
out / all night in the pantry

It took some doing / to get it out
safe and ultrasound as / it kept banging
its fangs against windows / and screening
swooping here and there as if / it knew
what it wanted but not how to get it
/ searching for something the pantry did
not / have nor the kitchen nor the house
nor the / woods nor the world as it
flitted upon / rosy dawn air on down
Sherwood Road toward / Buggytop Trail
and home to Lost Cove Cave.

CODA

THE NEXT GENERATION

—*after Li Bai*

The cicadas have left their forms behind,
      going back underground.
Only the hawks' screams float on the wind,
      teaching the next generation.

No longer tired, I look at Stone Nest;
      Stone Nest looks at me.
I sit and sit on the mountaintop;
      the mountaintop sits on me.

We chant in silent emptiness.
Soon there is only Stone Nest.

NOTES

TITLE
This collection is divided into two parts—Peakless Mountain and Shoreless River—these being the two parts of the name of the Zen temple that I have served as abbot since 2016: Muhozan Kozenji. The New Orleans Zen Temple is located on the shoreless river of the Mississippi, while its more recent counterpart, Stone Nest Zen Dojo, is located on the peakless mountain of the Cumberland Plateau in Tennessee. The many poems that are "after" Chinese poets are intended as intimate conversations with the dead over time and space.

PROEM: LEAVING THE ABBOT BEHIND (17)
After Du Fu, "Parting from Abbot Zan."
http://www.chinese-poems.com/d49.html

FORMLESS MERIT (21)
The "gentle torture of being / time" is a reference to Eihei Dōgen's "Uji" ("Time-Being") in his *Shobogenzo* (*Treasury of the True Dharma Eye*). In a famous koan, when asked the meaning of Bodhidharma's coming from the West, Joshu answers, "The oak tree in the garden."

SEMIS CLIMB THE MOUNTAIN ROAD (23)
After Liu Chih, "Tune: Sheep on the Mountain Slope" from *Chinese Poetry: An Anthology of Modes and Genres*, edited by Wai-Lim Yip (Duke University Press, 1997), 348–9.

WIND FLOWS OVER STONE NEST DOJO (24)
After Huang Tingjian, "Poem on the Hall of Pines and Wind."
https://learning.hku.hk/ccch9051/group-24/items/show/44

WRITTEN FOR THE BACKYARD NATURALIST FROM MAINE (30)
After Du Fu, "Written for Scholar Wei."
http://www.chinese-poems.com/d20.html

IN THE POSTURE OF THE WATER DRAGON (31)
After Wang Wei, "Stopping at the Incense Storing Temple."
http://www.chinese-poems.com/incense.html
Born in 1952, I identify with my Chinese zodiac sign, the Water
Dragon.

AS UNATTACHED AS LEAVES IN OCTOBER (32)
Bai Juyi: "I sit up all night in zazen / yet autumn can still bring a
sudden sigh / two last ties / otherwise / nothing obstructs this
mind of mine."

THE SAMADHI OF WORDS (33)
Bai Juyi: "After deep study of the empty dharma / all life's flora
has fallen away / all but the demon poetry / a glimpse of wind or
moon, and, ugh, I'm at it again." Additional commentary on this
poem can be found at https://www.neworleanszentemple.org/
new-blog/the-way-of-the-way.

SOMETHING FOR SU TUNGPO (34)
This poem, published in 1999, is the distant precursor of the oth-
er, more recent conversations with Chinese poets in this volume.
It was written during a feverish bout with the flu while reading
Lin Yutang's Gay Genius: The Life and Times of Su Tungpo (1947).

AFTER HARD RAIN (36)
After Du Fu, "Clearing Rain."
http://www.chinese-poems.com/d13.html

PETRICHOR (38)
Written during the California drought of 2015, said to be the
worst in history, this poem accompanies my "planting" of a Zen
xeriscape in Bakersfield.

THE TEACHER KEEPS HIS COUNSEL (41)
After Wang Wei, "Replying to Subprefect Zhang."
http://www.chinese-poems.com/zhang.html

I CLIMB STONE NEST IN SILENCE (42)
After Li Yu, "I Climb the Western Tower in Silence."
http://www.chinese-poems.com/sickle.html

OUT WITH THE OLD (45)
After Su Shi (Su Tungpo), "New Year's Watch."
http://www.chinese-poems.com/su2.html

THE ZEN MONK TO HIS DESIGNER DOG (46)
Perhaps the most famous koan, the first in the collection called
The Gateless Gate (Mumonkan), asks: "Does a dog have Buddha
nature?" And Joshu answers cryptically, "Wu! (not)." We must
all decide for ourselves.

STILL LIFES EVERYWHERE (47)
Perhaps Henry Miller's best book title: *Stand Still Like the
Hummingbird* (1962).

NIGHTTIME THOUGHTS ON THE MOUNTAIN (50)
After Du Fu, "Nocturnal Reflections While Traveling."
http://www.chinese-poems.com/d01.html

THE PAST IS NOT PAST IN SEWANEE, TENNESSEE (53)
After Huang Tingjian, "Clear Bright," *Love and the Turning Year:
One Hundred More Poems from the Chinese,* translated by Ken-
neth Rexroth (New York: New Directions, 1970), p. 90. The Qing
Ming or Clear Brightness Festival is China's Day of the Dead,
devoted to commemorating nature and the ancestors. The first
day of the festival is called Tomb Sweeping Day.

DEEP SPRING RAIN HAS PASSED (54)
After Ouyang Xiu, "Deep in Spring, the Rain's Passed (Picking
Mulberries)."
http://www.chinese-poems.com/oyx2.html

RETURNING TO LIVE IN THE SOUTH (55)
After Tao Qian, "Returning to Live in the South."
http://www.chinese-poems.com/young.html

THE VIEW FROM MY WINDOW (56)
After Wang Wei, "Huazi Ridge."
http://www.chinese-poems.com/ww2.html

OLD STONES, NEW BUDDHAS (58)
The voluminous sleeves of the monastic's black robes or koromo
have been compared to bats' or birds' wings.

DARUMA GETS HIS EARS CLEANED (68)
Daruma (Bodhidharma) getting his ears cleaned is a common
motif in Japanese sumi-e painting and netsuke. It is just one of
many depictions of the formidable founder of Zen in compro-
mising situations. This vulnerability is what makes him perhaps
more accessible and down-to-earth than the more spiritually
aloof Buddha. See H. Neill McFarland's *Daruma: The Founder of
Japanese Zen in Art and Popular Culture* (Kodansha, 1987).

NO LONGER DRUNK ON THE ROAD AT NIGHT (69)
After Li Yu, "Last Night the Wind and Rain Together Blew (Crows
Crying at Night)."
http://www.chinese-poems.com/y8.html

DRINKING WINE AT STONE NEST (70)
After Tao Qin, "Drinking Wine."
http://www.chinese-poems.com/wine.html

A KAYAK ON BAYOU ST. JOHN AT JAZZ FEST (71)
"A Light Boat with Short Oars (Picking Mulberries)."
http://www.chinese-poems.com/oyx1.html

SUNDAY PARTY BOAT, BAYOU ST. JOHN (72)
"A Painted Boat Carrying Wine (Picking Mulberries)."
http://www.chinese-poems.com/oyx3.html

IDLENESS (NESTING) (73)
After Li Yu, "Lazy," *Love and the Turning Year: One Hundred More Poems from the Chinese,* translated by Kenneth Rexroth (New York: New Directions, 1970), p. 102.

THE HERMIT PUTS OUT A MISSION STATEMENT (76)
For a quick (and quickening) tour of archaeology and speleology in Tennessee, see John Jeremiah Sullivan's "Unnamed Caves" in *Pulphead: Essays* (Farrar, Straus & Giroux, 2011).

MASTER TO MONKS (77)
Near the end of his life, I once thanked my Zen master for all he had taught me. He replied: "I haven't taught you anything."

THE MAN IN THE BLUE WHEELCHAIR (78)
I took care of my master for the last four years of his life. One day I entered his room and found him asleep in his wheelchair and was struck by the similarity of his posture to that of the figure in Picasso's *The Old Guitarist,* painted during the artist's Blue Period. "The Man with the Blue Guitar," a poem by Wallace Stevens based on Picasso's painting, naturally came to mind as well.

REMEMBERING REIBIN (80)
After Su Tungpo (Su Shi), "Remembering Min Ch'e: A Letter to his Brother Su Che," *Love and the Turning Year: One Hundred More Poems from the Chinese,* translated by Kenneth Rexroth (New York: New Directions, 1970), p. 89. For thirty years (1991–2021), the New Orleans Zen Temple was located at 748 Camp Street, formerly the site of Jazz City, the recording studio of Cosimo Matassa.

STILL MOURNING MY LATE ZEN MASTER (81)
After Meng Haoran, "To the Buddhist Priest Yuan from Chang-an." http://www.chinese-poems.com/m10.html

THERE'S SOMETHING ABOUT BAMBOO (83)
Robert Livingston was an eminent member of the American Bamboo Society. In his prime, he was a force of nature who, like

bamboo, was difficult to restrain. His neighbors compared him to Nosferatu because of his shaved head, his pointed ears, and the fears he inspired when they complained about the bamboo burrowing under the property lines. He always dressed in black.

TO THE ASHES OF MY MASTER ON THE ALTAR (84)
Robert Livingston's dharma names, Taikaku Reibin, mean Great Palace and Spiritual Vivacity. After his cremation, his daughter said that she imagined each of his ashes in the urn sitting erect in zazen.

MI FU BOWING TO THE STONE (89)
Mi Fu (米黻) or Mi Fei (米芾) (1051–1107) was an eccentric Chinese painter, poet, and calligrapher of the Song Dynasty, and friend of Su Tungpo (Su Shi). As a painter, he was known for his misty landscapes. As a subject for painting, he is often depicted bowing to a huge stone in the garden, which he was known to address as his elder brother.

THE DEATH OF TWO POSSUMS (95)
Readers of Thomas Hardy's poetry may be reminded of the stanzaic form in his famous poem on the wreck of *Titanic*, "The Convergence of the Twain." The shape of the stanzas mimics a ship or a glacier on the ocean's horizon, or in this case, possums and cars on the road. The koan of "two arrows meeting" is a rich and multivalent image in Zen literature, while "the end is important in all things" comes from *Hagakure*, the eighteenth-century *Book of the Samurai*.

THE CHANGING LIGHT AT STONE NEST (102)
This poem deserves some context behind its creation. Back in the 1990s, while living in Romania, I wrote an essay on James Merrill's novel, *The (Diblos) Notebook*, which is set in Greece. I delivered an early version as a paper at a conference in Thessaloniki before it was published in the proceedings. ["The Poet's Novel as Komboloi: James Merrill's *The (Diblos) Notebook*," *Hellenism and the U.S.: Constructions and*

Deconstructions, edited by Savas Patsalidas (Thessaloniki: Aristotle University, 1994).] I submitted the essay first, though, to *The Yale Review*. The editor, J. D. McClatchy, rejected the essay but sent it to Merrill, who graciously replied with an appreciative note on one of his photo-postcards, thanking me for my attention to his "youthful novel." One morning recently, during zazen, as I observed the changing light in the winter woods outside the dojo at Stone Nest, I thought of Merrill and his monumental poem *The Changing Light at Sandover*. After zazen, I found my copy on a shelf and leafed through it, surprised to find that I had, evident by my underlinings and marginal notes, read all six hundred pages. This poem, written around his fascination and conversations with a homemade OUIJA board and in which Blake plays a major role, is a unique and epic *jeu d'esprit* of American poetry. It occurred to me that my marginalia might continue the conversation with dead poets, just as other poems here converse with the ancient Chinese. Thus came about this experiment ("absurd gobbledygook, funny if you follow," as I noted in pencil in the endpapers of Merrill's masterwork), an assemblage consisting of my marginal notes (in italics) interspersed with my present-day observations on the changing light at Stone Nest.

BEYOND THE BEYOND (106)
The closing mantra of the Hannya Shingyo (Heart Sutra)—*gya tei gya tei hara so gya tei boji so waka*—means approximately: "Go, go, go beyond, go together beyond the beyond, to the shore of satori."

A BAT IN THE PANTRY (108)
See the note above on "The Hermit Puts Out a Mission Statement," page 76.

THE NEXT GENERATION (112)
After Li Bai, "Sitting Alone on Mount Jingting Shan Hill." http://www.chinese-poems.com/lb9.html

RICHARD COLLINS taught at universities in the United States, Wales, Romania, and Bulgaria before retiring as Dean Emeritus of Arts and Humanities at California State University Bakersfield. He spent a decade at Louisiana State University (where he was the first faculty advisor for *New Delta Review*) and a decade at Xavier University of Louisiana (where he edited the *Xavier Review*). He has been a Fulbright researcher in London and Fulbright senior lecturer at the Universities of Bucharest and Timişoara, as well as a Leverhulme Fellow in Wales. He has translated poetry from Romanian and books from French, including Taisen Deshimaru's *Autobiography of a Zen Monk* (Hohm Press, 2022) and Philippe Coupey's *Zen Fragments: Teachings and Reflections of a Zen Monk in Paris* (Hohm Press, 2024). He also edited Deshimaru's *Mushotoku Mind: The Heart of the Heart Sutra* (Hohm Presss, 2012). His own books include *John Fante: A Literary Portrait* (Guernica Editions, 2000), *No Fear Zen: Discovering Balance in an Unbalanced World* (Hohm Press, 2015), and *In Search of the Hermaphrodite: A Memoir* (Tough Poets Press, 2024). Since 2016 he has been abbot of the New Orleans Zen Temple and now resides in Sewanee, Tennessee, where he directs Stone Nest Zen Dojo.

SHANTI ARTS

NATURE ▪ ART ▪ SPIRIT

Please visit us online
to browse our entire book catalog,
including poetry collections and fiction,
books on travel, nature, healing, art,
photography, and more.

Also take a look at our highly regarded art
and literary journal, *Still Point Arts Quarterly*,
which may be downloaded for free.

www.shantiarts.com

www.ingramcontent.com/pod-product-compliance
Lightning Source LLC
Chambersburg PA
CBHW070333090426
42733CB00012B/2466